Roderick Dockery   *Chris Mcbride*

ABOUT US

Bossing Up: Thriving as a Young Man Raised by a Single Parent" was created to shatter the stereotypes and statistics surrounding young men raised by single parents. Rather than succumbing to the odds, this book aims to empower and inspire young men to thrive in spite of their circumstances.

With personal stories, testimonials, and expert guidance, this book provides young men with the tools and strategies to build resilience, forge strong relationships, plan their careers, and overcome adversity. It emphasizes the importance of understanding and addressing the unique challenges faced by young men raised by single parents, and provides actionable steps to help readers achieve their goals.

By sharing the triumphs and struggles of other young men who have faced similar challenges, "Bossing Up" reminds readers that they are not alone and that success is possible with determination and the right mindset. The book also advocates for mental health awareness and support for grieving families, providing a holistic approach to navigating life's challenges.

Overall, "Bossing Up" was created to serve as a trusty sidekick for young men raised by single parents, guiding them through life's obstacles and empowering them to create a future they can be proud of.

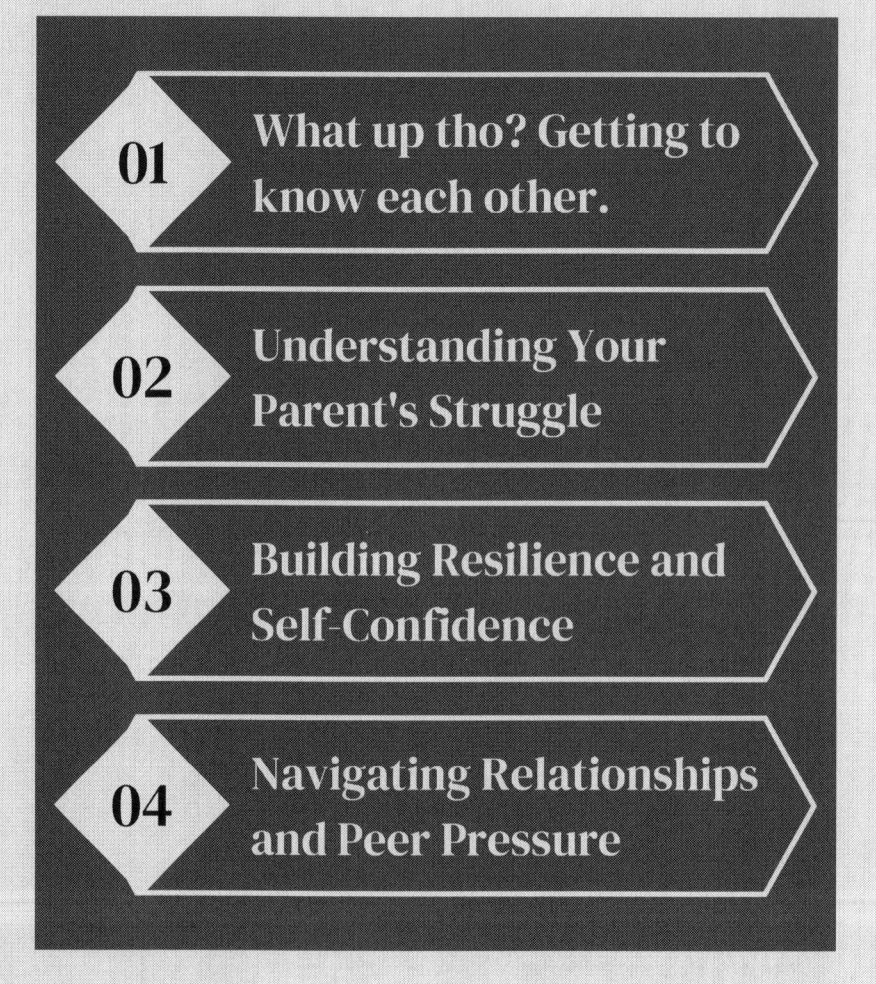

TABLE OF CONTENTS

01 What up tho? Getting to know each other.

02 Understanding Your Parent's Struggle

03 Building Resilience and Self-Confidence

04 Navigating Relationships and Peer Pressure

TABLE OF CONTENTS

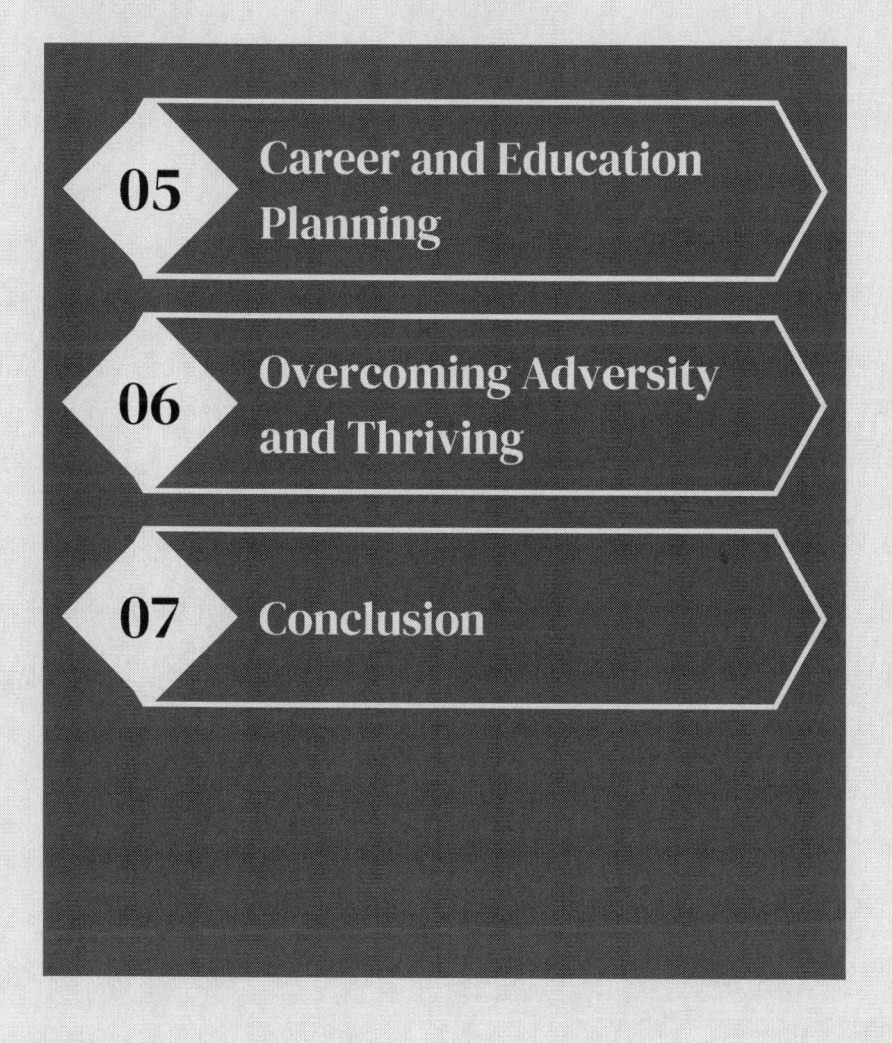

05 — Career and Education Planning

06 — Overcoming Adversity and Thriving

07 — Conclusion

Chapter #1 What up tho? Getting to know each other.

Chapter 1: What up tho? Getting to know each other.

Welcome to "Bossing Up: Thriving as a Young Man Raised by a Single Parent"! You might be wondering what this program is all about, and why you should even care. Well, buckle up, because we're about to embark on a journey that will open your eyes, challenge your beliefs, and inspire you to become the best version of yourself. Trust us; you're in for a wild ride.

We've all heard the statistics and stereotypes about young men raised by single parents – the increased likelihood of dropping out of school, facing emotional and financial struggles, and a higher risk of getting involved in crime. But let's set the record straight: those are only part of the story. We're here to shatter the mold, defy the odds, and show you that you can not only survive but thrive as a young man raised by a single parent.

Understanding the unique challenges faced by young men like you is crucial to overcoming them. It's like playing a video game with a guidebook – you'll still face obstacles, but you'll be better equipped to tackle them head-on. And that's what we're here for – to provide you with the tools, strategies, and insights to help you succeed.

Chapter 1: What up tho? Getting to know each other.

This ebook will be your trusty sidekick, guiding you through the intricacies of building resilience, forging strong relationships, planning your career, and overcoming adversity. Our mission is to help you navigate life's challenges and emerge victorious – or, as we like to say, "boss up" and create a future you can be proud of.

Now, let's kick things off with some personal stories and testimonials from young men who have faced similar challenges and come out on top. These tales of triumph are here to remind you that you're not alone, and that with determination and the right mindset, anything is possible.

Meet Alex, a young man who grew up with his single mother and two siblings in a low-income neighborhood. While his friends were drawn into a life of crime and drugs, Alex chose a different path. He dedicated himself to his education, worked part-time to help support his family, and spent his free time volunteering at a local community center. Through hard work and perseverance, Alex earned a full scholarship to a prestigious university and is now a successful software engineer.

Chapter 1: What up tho? Getting to know each other.

Or how about David, who was raised by his single father after losing his mother to a terminal illness? David struggled with grief and isolation, but instead of succumbing to despair, he found solace in music. He taught himself to play the guitar and started a band with his friends. Today, David is an accomplished musician with several albums under his belt, and he uses his platform to advocate for mental health awareness and support for grieving families.

These inspiring stories are just the tip of the iceberg. Throughout this ebook, you'll encounter more accounts of young men defying the odds and thriving in spite of their circumstances. Let these stories be a beacon of hope, a reminder that you, too, can achieve greatness if you believe in yourself and take action.

To sum it up, in this introductory chapter, we welcome you to the program, discuss the challenges faced by young men raised by single parents, and emphasize the importance of understanding and addressing these challenges. We also provide an overview of the ebook's content and share personal stories and testimonials to inspire and motivate you.

Chapter 1: What up tho? Getting to know each other.

So, are you ready to embark on this life-changing journey? Are you prepared to embrace your inner boss, conquer your fears, and shape your destiny? If the answer is yes, then let's dive right in. Together, we'll navigate the complex, exhilarating, and sometimes downright hilarious world of growing up as a young man raised by a single parent.

In the words of the immortal Ferris Bueller, "Life moves pretty fast. If you don't stop and look around once in a while, you could miss it." So, let's not waste another moment – it's time to boss up and create the life you deserve.

Welcome aboard, and let the adventure begin!

"Bossing Up: Thriving as a Young Man Raised by a Single Parent" Chapter 1: Introduction
Fill in the blank:

We're here to shatter the mold, defy the odds, and show you that you can not only survive but _____ as a young man raised by a single parent."

In the words of Ferris Bueller, "Life moves pretty fast. If you don't stop and look around once in a while, you could _____."

This ebook will be your trusty _____, guiding you through the intricacies of building resilience, forging strong relationships, planning your career, and overcoming adversity.

Multiple Choice:
What is one of the main goals of this ebook?
a. To entertain you with humorous stories
b. To provide tools, strategies, and insights to help you succeed
c. To teach you how to become an expert in a specific field
d. To promote a specific political agenda

Journaling:
Reflect on a personal challenge you have faced as a young man raised by a single parent. How did you overcome it, or what steps can you take to overcome it in the future? Write a short paragraph about your experience.

True or False:
This ebook will only focus on the negative aspects of growing up with a single parent.

Multiple Choice:
Which of the following is NOT an example of a young man thriving as mentioned in the introduction?
a. Alex, who earned a full scholarship to a prestigious university and became a successful software engineer
b. David, who became an accomplished musician and mental health advocate
c. John, who gave up on his dreams and blamed his upbringing for his failures
d. Both Alex and David are examples of young men thriving

Chapter #2 Understanding Your Parent's Struggle

Chapter #2 Understanding Your Parent's Struggle

Picture this: you're watching an intense tennis match between two world-class players, and the ball is being volleyed back and forth at lightning speed. Now imagine trying to keep up with that ball while juggling flaming torches, balancing on a tightrope, and solving a Rubik's Cube. Sounds impossible, right? Well, that's a pretty accurate representation of what it's like to be a single parent.

In this chapter, we'll dive into the nitty-gritty of the challenges faced by single parents and explore the impact of these struggles on the parent-child relationship. We'll also provide you with strategies for effective communication and relationship-building, backed by expert advice from psychologists and family therapists. So grab your scuba gear, and let's take the plunge into the complex, emotionally charged world of single parenthood.

Chapter #2 Understanding Your Parent's Struggle

Let's start by examining the most common challenges faced by single parents:

Financial Difficulties: Money might not buy happiness, but it certainly helps pay the bills. Single parents often struggle to make ends meet, juggling the costs of housing, food, clothing, and education on a single income. This financial strain can lead to a constant state of stress and anxiety, impacting their mental health and overall well-being.

Time Management: Time is a precious commodity, and for single parents, it's often in short supply. Between working long hours, managing household chores, and attending to their children's needs, single parents have to stretch themselves thin to keep everything running smoothly. This constant race against the clock can lead to burnout and negatively affect their emotional state.

Chapter #2 Understanding Your Parent's Struggle

Emotional Stress: Single parents bear the full weight of their family's emotional well-being, which can be overwhelming. They may feel guilty about not being able to provide their children with a two-parent home, struggle with feelings of loneliness and isolation, and face judgment or stigma from society. This emotional burden can take a significant toll on their mental health and relationships.

Now that we've laid out the challenges, let's explore how they impact the parent-child relationship:

Limited Quality Time: With so much on their plate, single parents may struggle to find the time and energy to bond with their children. This lack of quality time can lead to feelings of disconnection and misunderstandings between parent and child.

Heightened Stress Levels: A stressed-out parent is more likely to be irritable, impatient, or emotionally unavailable, which can strain the parent-child relationship. Children may feel that they are walking on eggshells around their parent, creating an atmosphere of tension and unease.

Chapter #2 Understanding Your Parent's Struggle

Role Strain: In single-parent households, children may take on additional responsibilities to help ease their parent's burden. While this can foster a sense of maturity and independence, it can also blur the lines between parent and child roles, leading to confusion and conflicts.

Now that we've painted a picture of the challenges faced by single parents and their impact on the parent-child relationship, it's time to shift gears and focus on the importance of empathy and support. When you understand and acknowledge the struggles your parent is facing, you can begin to foster a more compassionate, supportive, and nurturing environment for both of you. As the saying goes, "A problem shared is a problem halved."

Here are some strategies for communicating effectively with your parent and building a strong, positive relationship:

Active Listening: When your parent is sharing their feelings or concerns, give them your undivided attention. Put away distractions like your phone, maintain eye contact, and listen without interrupting. This simple act of active listening can create a powerful connection and show your parent that you genuinely care.

Chapter #2 Understanding Your Parent's Struggle

Open and Honest Communication: Be open and honest about your own feelings, needs, and concerns. Encourage your parent to do the same, and create a safe space where both of you can express yourselves without fear of judgment or criticism. This open line of communication will help to build trust and mutual understanding.

Show Appreciation: Express gratitude for the sacrifices your parent makes and the hard work they put in to provide for you. A heartfelt "thank you" or a simple hug can go a long way in making your parent feel valued and appreciated.

Offer Support: Offer to help with household chores or other tasks to lighten your parent's load. This gesture not only eases their burden but also demonstrates your commitment to working together as a team.

To further strengthen the parent-child relationship, we've enlisted the help of expert psychologists and family therapists for their advice:

Create Shared Rituals: Establishing routines or rituals, like a weekly game night or a daily walk together, can help create a sense of stability and connection. These shared experiences can become cherished memories and strengthen your bond.

Chapter #2 Understanding Your Parent's Struggle

Practice Empathy: Put yourself in your parent's shoes and try to understand their perspective. This exercise in empathy can help you be more compassionate and supportive in your interactions.

Set Boundaries: Establish clear boundaries between parent and child roles to maintain a healthy balance in your relationship. While it's essential to support each other, it's equally important to recognize and respect each other's roles and responsibilities.

Seek Professional Help: If you and your parent are struggling to navigate your relationship, consider seeking the guidance of a family therapist or counselor. These professionals can provide valuable insights and tools to help you build a stronger, healthier bond.

In this chapter, we've delved into the challenges faced by single parents, explored the impact of these struggles on the parent-child relationship, and emphasized the importance of empathy and support. We've also provided strategies for effective communication and relationship-building, backed by expert advice from psychologists and family therapists.

Chapter #2 Understanding Your Parent's Struggle

By understanding your parent's struggles and implementing these strategies, you'll be well on your way to fostering a strong, positive, and loving relationship that will serve as a foundation for your growth and success. So, as you continue on this journey, remember the wise words of author Leo Buscaglia: "Too often, we underestimate the power of a touch, a smile, a kind word, a listening ear, an honest compliment, or the smallest act of caring, all of which have the potential to turn a life around."

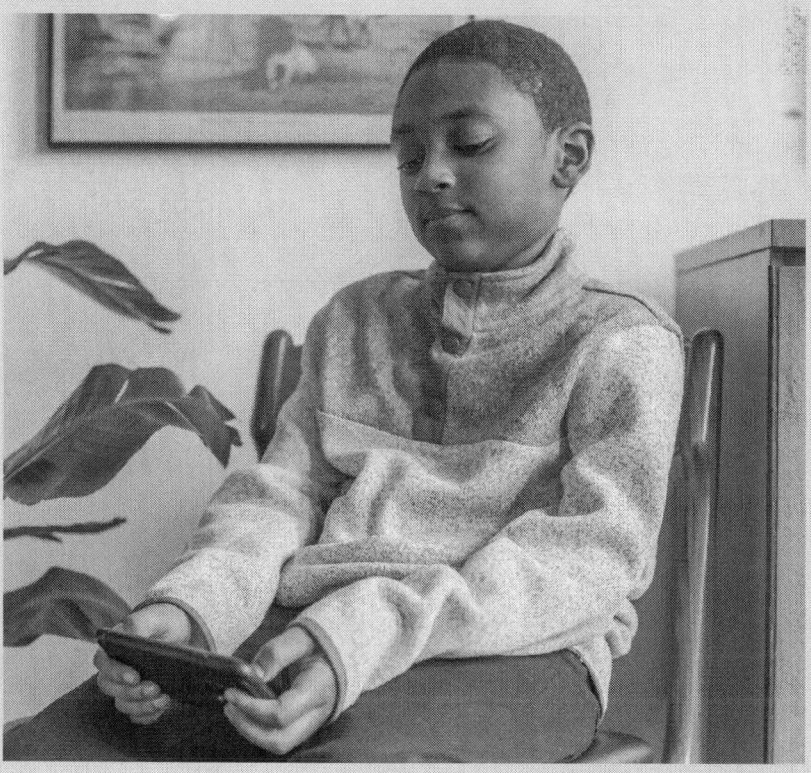

"Bossing Up: Thriving as a Young Man Raised by a Single Parent" Workbook - Chapter 2: Understanding Your Parent's Struggle

Fill in the blank:

Single parents often struggle to make ends meet, juggling the costs of housing, food, clothing, and _____ on a single income.

Multiple Choice:
Which of the following is NOT a common challenge faced by single parents?
a. Financial Difficulties
b. Time Management
c. Emotional Stress
d. Boredom

Journaling:
Write a paragraph about a time when you noticed your parent struggling with one of the challenges mentioned in this chapter. How did it make you feel, and how do you think you can support them in the future?

True or False:
A stressed-out parent is more likely to be irritable, impatient, or emotionally unavailable, which can strain the parent-child relationship.

Fill in the blank:
When you understand and acknowledge the struggles your parent is facing, you can begin to foster a more _____, _____, and nurturing environment for both of you.

Multiple Choice:
Which of the following is NOT a strategy for communicating effectively with your parent and building a strong, positive relationship?
a. Active Listening
b. Open and Honest Communication
c. Ignoring their feelings
d. Show Appreciation

Matching:
Match the following expert advice with their correct descriptions.

A. Create Shared Rituals   1. Try to understand your parent's perspective
B. Practice Empathy   2. Establish clear boundaries between parent and child roles
C. Set Boundaries   3. Establish routines or rituals that you can do together
D. Seek Professional Help   4. Consider seeking the guidance of a family therapist or counselor

Fill in the blank:
"Too often, we underestimate the power of a _____, a _____, a _____, a _____, an _____, or the _____, all of which have the potential to turn a life around." – Leo Buscaglia

Chapter #3 Building Resilience and Self-Confidence

Chapter #3 Building Resilience and Self-Confidence

Imagine you're watching a high-stakes poker game in a dimly lit room. The tension is palpable as each player carefully considers their next move. Suddenly, one player pushes all of their chips into the center of the table, confidently declaring, "All in." That player, my friend, is the embodiment of resilience and self-confidence. And guess what? That player can be you.

In this chapter, we'll explore the unique challenges faced by young men raised by single parents and provide you with the tools and strategies to build your resilience and self-confidence like a master poker player. We'll also share personal stories and testimonials from individuals who have overcome adversity and expert advice from psychologists and life coaches. So grab your sunglasses and poker face, and let's dive in.

Chapter #3 Building Resilience and Self-Confidence

First, let's identify the specific challenges faced by young men raised by single parents:

Isolation: Growing up in a single-parent household can sometimes be a lonely experience. Without a second parent or siblings, young men may feel isolated and struggle to find a sense of belonging.

Stigma: Society often perpetuates stereotypes about single-parent families, leading to feelings of shame or stigma. This negative perception can chip away at a young man's self-esteem and sense of self-worth.

Low Self-Esteem: The combined impact of isolation, stigma, and a potentially strained parent-child relationship can contribute to low self-esteem. This lack of self-confidence can hinder personal growth, hinder relationships, and limit a young man's potential.

Now that we've identified the challenges, it's time to stack the deck in your favor with strategies for building resilience and self-confidence

Chapter #3 Building Resilience and Self-Confidence

Set SMART Goals: Establish Specific, Measurable, Achievable, Relevant, and Time-bound (SMART) goals to give yourself a clear sense of direction and purpose. Break down larger goals into smaller, manageable steps, and celebrate your progress along the way.

Practice Self-Care: Prioritize your physical, emotional, and mental well-being by adopting a self-care routine. Exercise regularly, eat a balanced diet, get enough sleep, and engage in activities that bring you joy and relaxation.

Surround Yourself with Positive Influences: Build a support network of friends, mentors, and role models who encourage, uplift, and inspire you. Positive influences can help counteract feelings of isolation and stigma, and provide guidance and motivation when the going gets tough.

Embrace Failure as a Learning Opportunity: Develop a growth mindset by recognizing that failure is a natural part of the learning process. Instead of dwelling on setbacks, analyze what went wrong and use those lessons to improve and grow

Chapter #3 Building Resilience and Self-Confidence

Cultivate Gratitude: Focus on the positives in your life by practicing gratitude regularly. Acknowledging your blessings can shift your perspective and improve your overall sense of self-worth and happiness.

To further illustrate the power of resilience and self-confidence, let's explore some personal stories and testimonials from young men who have triumphed over adversity

John, a college student raised by a single mother, faced feelings of isolation and low self-esteem throughout his teenage years. However, by setting SMART goals and surrounding himself with positive influences, he overcame these challenges and found his path to success. Today, John is a proud member of his university's debate team, actively involved in community service, and has a close-knit circle of friends who support and inspire him.

Michael, another young man raised by a single parent, struggled with the stigma associated with single-parent families. He began practicing self-care and cultivating gratitude to shift his mindset and build his self-confidence. As a result, Michael discovered a newfound sense of self-worth and now uses his experiences to mentor other young men facing similar challenges.

Chapter #3 Building Resilience and Self-Confidence

Expert advice from psychologists and life coaches can also provide valuable insights into building resilience and self-confidence

Practice Mindfulness: Engage in mindfulness techniques, such as meditation, deep breathing exercises, or journaling, to help you stay present and focused. Mindfulness can reduce stress, improve emotional regulation, and increase self-awareness.

Develop Assertiveness: Learn to assert yourself and communicate your needs and boundaries effectively. Being assertive can help you build self-confidence and improve your relationships with others.

Challenge Negative Thoughts: Identify and challenge negative thought patterns that may be holding you back. Replace self-defeating thoughts with positive affirmations and self-compassion.

Seek Professional Guidance: If you're struggling to build resilience and self-confidence, consider working with a therapist or life coach. They can provide personalized guidance, support, and strategies to help you overcome challenges and reach your full potential.

Chapter #3 Building Resilience and Self-Confidence

In this chapter, we've discussed the unique challenges faced by young men raised by single parents and provided strategies for building resilience and self-confidence. By setting SMART goals, practicing self-care, surrounding yourself with positive influences, embracing failure as a learning opportunity, and cultivating gratitude, you can build a strong foundation for success. Personal stories and testimonials from individuals who have triumphed over adversity, as well as expert advice from psychologists and life coaches, offer additional inspiration and guidance. Remember, with the right tools and mindset, you can confidently push all your chips into the center of the table and win big in the game of life.

Chapter 3 Workbook: Building Resilience and Self-Confidence

Fill in the blanks:

Set _____ Goals to give yourself a clear sense of direction and purpose.

Practice _____ to prioritize your physical, emotional, and mental well-being.

Surround yourself with _____ influences to counteract feelings of isolation and stigma.

Embrace failure as a _____ opportunity.

Cultivate _____ to improve your overall sense of self-worth and happiness.

Multiple choice selection:
Which of the following is NOT a challenge faced by young men raised by single parents?
a. Isolation
b. Stigma
c. Procrastination
d. Low Self-Esteem

Journaling:
Reflect on a personal setback or failure you've experienced. How can you use the lessons learned from that experience to build resilience and self-confidence moving forward?

Identify a SMART goal you'd like to achieve. Break it down into smaller, manageable steps, and outline a plan to achieve it.

List three positive influences in your life (friends, mentors, role models) and describe how they encourage, uplift, and inspire you.

Practice gratitude: Write down five things you are grateful for today.

Chapter 4: Navigating Relationships and Peer Pressure

Chapter 4: Navigating Relationships and Peer Pressure

Navigating the complex world of relationships and peer pressure is no easy task, especially for teenage boys. With raging hormones, changing bodies, and a developing sense of self, the pressures to conform and fit in can be overwhelming. But fear not! In this witty and engaging chapter, we will delve into the impact of peer pressure on teenage boys, offering strategies for resisting negative influences, and providing tips for building positive relationships with peers and mentors. Let's dive into this enlightening and motivational journey, filled with personal stories, expert advice, and a healthy dose of humor.

The Impact of Peer Pressure on Teenage Boys.

Teenage boys are often bombarded with conflicting messages from friends, family, and society, leading to a roller coaster of emotions and confusion. Peer pressure can take many forms, from subtle nudges to outright coercion, and can influence everything from clothing choices to risky behavior. In this section, we will explore the profound impact of peer pressure on teenage boys and provide insights into how they can recognize and resist negative influences.

Chapter 4: Navigating Relationships and Peer Pressure

Strategies for Resisting Negative Influences:

Armed with a better understanding of the impact of peer pressure, it's time to empower our teenage boys with strategies for resisting negative influences. From practicing assertiveness and developing self-awareness to finding positive role models and pursuing personal interests, this section offers practical and progressive advice that will encourage young men to be true to themselves. Along the way, we'll share captivating and relatable stories of individuals who have successfully navigated the treacherous waters of peer pressure, offering hope and inspiration to readers.

Tips for Building Positive Relationships with Peers and Mentors. Strong, positive relationships with peers and mentors can be a lifeline for teenage boys, helping them navigate the challenges of adolescence and develop a healthy sense of self. In this section, we'll provide tips for building these connections, from seeking out like-minded individuals to engaging in extracurricular activities that foster collaboration and camaraderie. We'll also discuss the importance of mentors in guiding young men towards success and personal growth, and share inspiring stories of mentor-mentee relationships that have made a lasting impact.

Chapter 4: Navigating Relationships and Peer Pressure

The Importance of Communication Skills and Boundary-Setting in Relationships:
Communication is the key to any successful relationship, and teenage boys are no exception. This section delves into the art of communication, exploring techniques for expressing thoughts and emotions effectively, as well as listening actively and empathetically. We'll also emphasize the importance of boundary-setting in relationships, equipping young men with the tools to assert their needs and protect their emotional well-being. Throughout this section, we'll share humorous and relatable anecdotes that demonstrate the power of communication and boundary-setting in action.

Personal Stories and Testimonials. A picture may be worth a thousand words, but personal stories and testimonials can be even more powerful in inspiring change. In this section, we've compiled a diverse array of stories from teenage boys and young men who have overcome peer pressure and built healthy relationships. These riveting accounts will offer readers a glimpse into the lives of others who have faced similar challenges, providing encouragement and hope for those who may be struggling themselves.

Chapter 4: Navigating Relationships and Peer Pressure

Expert Advice from Psychologists and Educators:
To wrap up this comprehensive guide, we've enlisted the help of psychologists and educators to provide expert advice on navigating relationships and peer pressure. Their insights, drawn from years of experience working with adolescents, will help equip young men with the knowledge and skills necessary to forge a path towards healthy relationships and personal growth. These experts will share their electrifying wisdom on topics such as self-esteem, emotional intelligence, and conflict resolution, offering a progressive and well-rounded approach to tackling the challenges of adolescence.

As we reach the end of this inspiring journey, we hope that teenage boys, as well as their parents, teachers, and mentors, will feel better equipped to navigate the turbulent waters of relationships and peer pressure. This chapter has aimed to be not only enlightening and motivational but also engaging and relatable. With a blend of expert advice, personal stories, and practical strategies, we hope to have sparked a sense of empowerment and resilience in our readers. So, as you venture forth into the world of teenage relationships, remember to stay true to yourself, communicate openly, and surround yourself with positive influences. Your future self will thank you.

Chapter 4: Navigating Relationships and Peer Pressure

Fill in the blanks:
Peer pressure can take many forms, from _____ nudges to outright _____.

Strong, _____ relationships with peers and mentors can help teenage boys navigate the challenges of adolescence.

Communication is the _____ to any successful relationship.

The importance of _____-setting in relationships helps to assert needs and protect emotional well-being.

Multiple choice selection:
Which of the following is NOT a strategy for resisting negative influences?
a. Practicing assertiveness
b. Developing self-awareness
c. Gossiping about others
d. Pursuing personal interests

Journaling exercise:
Reflect on a time when you experienced peer pressure. How did you react, and what did you learn from the experience?

Role models and mentors:
Make a list of at least three role models or mentors in your life. Describe the qualities you admire in each of them and how they have influenced you positively.

Boundary-setting:
Write down three personal boundaries you would like to establish in your relationships. Explain why these boundaries are important to you.

Communication practice:
Choose a recent conversation where you experienced a misunderstanding or conflict. Analyze the situation and identify one thing you could have done differently to improve communication.

Chapter 5: Career and Education Planning

Chapter 5: Career and Education Planning

Planning for a successful career and education can seem like a daunting task, but fear not! In this witty and engaging chapter, we'll explore strategies for developing a career plan, building skills for success, and navigating the college application process. With a blend of personal stories, expert advice, and a healthy dose of humor, we aim to enlighten, motivate, and inspire young men to take control of their educational and career journeys.

Strategies for Developing a Career Plan and Building Skills for Success. In this section, we'll dive into the nitty-gritty of career planning, discussing strategies to help young men create a clear roadmap for their professional futures. We'll explore the benefits of internships, volunteer work, and extracurricular activities, showcasing how these opportunities can help develop essential skills, build a strong network, and even uncover hidden passions. As we delve into these topics, we'll share captivating and relatable stories from individuals who have successfully navigated their career paths, offering insights and encouragement to our readers.

Chapter 5: Career and Education Planning

Tips for Navigating the College Application Process. Applying to college can be an emotional rollercoaster, but we're here to help make the ride a little smoother. In this section, we'll provide practical tips for navigating the college application process, from writing a persuasive personal statement to acing the interview. We'll also tackle the often-overwhelming topic of financial aid, offering guidance on finding scholarships and navigating the complex world of student loans. Throughout this section, we'll share humorous and relatable anecdotes from young men who have successfully traversed the college application process, providing inspiration and hope to readers. The Importance of Lifelong Learning and Continuous Skill-Building

In today's rapidly evolving world, the importance of lifelong learning and continuous skill-building cannot be overstated. In this profound and insightful section, we'll discuss how embracing a growth mindset can lead to personal and professional success, as well as the multitude of ways young men can continue to develop their skills and knowledge throughout their lives. From online courses and workshops to networking events and mentorships, we'll explore the myriad opportunities available for ongoing personal development.

Chapter 5: Career and Education Planning

Personal Stories and Testimonials
There's nothing quite as powerful as a personal story to inspire and motivate. In this section, we've compiled riveting and relatable testimonials from young men who have successfully pursued their education and career goals. These stories will offer readers a glimpse into the challenges, triumphs, and lessons learned by others who have walked a similar path, providing encouragement and inspiration to those embarking on their own journeys.

Expert Advice from Career Counselors and Educators. To round out this comprehensive guide, we've enlisted the help of career counselors and educators to provide expert advice on effective education and career planning. Drawing from their wealth of experience and knowledge, these experts will share electrifying wisdom on topics such as goal-setting, time management, and networking, offering readers a progressive and well-rounded approach to career and education planning.

Chapter 5: Career and Education Planning

As we reach the end of this engaging and enlightening journey, we hope that young men, as well as readers of all ages and backgrounds, feel empowered and equipped to take control of their educational and career paths. With a blend of practical tips, personal stories, and expert advice, this chapter has provided a solid foundation for developing a career plan, building essential skills, and navigating the complex world of education.

As you move forward, remember that success is not a destination, but a lifelong journey that requires dedication, resilience, and adaptability. Embrace the challenges and opportunities that come your way, and never stop learning and growing. The world is full of possibilities, and by taking charge of your education and career planning, you have the power to create a fulfilling and rewarding life. We wish you all the best on your journey, and remember, the sky's the limit!

Chapter 5 Workbook Activities:

Fill in the blanks:

The importance of ____ learning and continuous skill-building cannot be overstated.

Embracing a ____ mindset can lead to personal and professional success.

The college application process can be an emotional ____, but we're here to help make the ride a little smoother.

In today's rapidly evolving world, ____ opportunities for ongoing personal development are essential.

Multiple choice selection:
Which of the following is NOT a strategy for effective career planning?
a. Goal-setting
b. Procrastination
c. Networking
d. Time management

Journaling exercise:
Reflect on your career and education goals. What steps can you take to work towards these goals, and what challenges do you anticipate facing along the way?

Building a network:
Make a list of at least three people who could serve as valuable connections in your chosen field or industry. How can you reach out to these individuals and start building a professional relationship?

Skill-building activities:
Identify three skills you would like to improve or develop. Research opportunities for skill-building in your community or online, such as workshops, classes, or mentorship programs.

College application practice:
Write a brief outline for a personal statement that highlights your unique qualities, experiences, and aspirations. Consider how this statement can help you stand out in the college application process.

Chapter #6 Overcoming Adversity and Thriving

Chapter #6 Overcoming Adversity and Thriving

"Life is 10% what happens to you and 90% how you react to it." – Charles R. Swindoll

The path of life is never smooth or without obstacles. Overcoming adversity and thriving, despite the challenges we face, is a crucial skill for personal growth and success. This chapter delves into the importance of developing a growth mindset and cultivating resilience in the face of challenges. We'll explore strategies for overcoming adversity, tips for staying focused on your goals, and rising above difficult circumstances. You'll also find personal stories and testimonials of individuals who have triumphed over adversity, as well as expert advice from psychologists and life coaches. So buckle up and get ready for an emotional roller coaster filled with wit, inspiration, and insights that will help you navigate life's inevitable storms.

The Power of a Growth Mindset:
"Success is not final, failure is not fatal: It is the courage to continue that counts." – Winston Churchill
A growth mindset is the belief that our abilities and intelligence can be developed through dedication and hard work. By cultivating a growth mindset, we can stay resilient in the face of challenges and learn from our setbacks. Embracing a growth mindset means accepting that failure is a natural part of the learning process, and it doesn't define our worth or potential.

Chapter #6 Overcoming Adversity and Thriving

Embrace failure as a learning opportunity:
When we experience failure, it's easy to feel disheartened and defeated. However, adopting a growth mindset means recognizing that failure is a necessary step on the path to success. Instead of fearing failure, learn to view it as an opportunity to grow, adapt, and improve. Remember, if Thomas Edison had given up after his first failed experiment, we might still be living in a world without electric light.

Cultivate a love for learning. A growth mindset goes hand in hand with a genuine love for learning. By remaining curious and seeking new experiences, you'll be more inclined to take risks, embrace challenges, and grow from setbacks. So, never stop asking questions, exploring new ideas, and pushing the boundaries of your comfort zone.

Strategies for Overcoming Adversity. "No one is going to hand me success. I must go out and get it myself. That's why I'm here. To dominate. To conquer. Both the world and myself." – Unknown

Overcoming adversity takes time, patience, and a willingness to face your fears. The following strategies can help you maintain a positive attitude, seek support, and ultimately triumph over life's obstacles.

Chapter #6 Overcoming Adversity and Thriving

Seek support from others. No one goes through life without encountering adversity, and it's important to remember that you don't have to face it alone. Reach out to friends, family, or professional counselors for guidance, encouragement, and emotional support. Surrounding yourself with a strong support network can help you navigate through tough times and emerge stronger on the other side.

Maintain a positive attitude. While it's not always easy to remain optimistic in the face of adversity, maintaining a positive attitude can significantly impact your ability to overcome challenges. Focus on your strengths, celebrate your accomplishments, and practice gratitude. By fostering a positive mindset, you'll be better equipped to tackle obstacles and bounce back from setbacks.

Break challenges into smaller steps. Overcoming adversity can often seem overwhelming. To make it more manageable, break down your challenges into smaller, more achievable steps. By tackling one small task at a time, you'll build momentum and confidence, making it easier to stay focused on your larger goals.

Chapter #6 Overcoming Adversity and Thriving

Visualize success. Regularly visualize yourself achieving your goals, and let that image fuel your motivation and drive. This mental exercise can help you stay focused on the future and provide the inspiration needed to persevere through tough times.

Create a realistic plan of action. Having a solid plan in place can make it easier to stay focused on your goals, even in the face of adversity. Break down your goals into smaller milestones, and outline the specific steps you'll need to take to achieve them. As you progress, regularly review and adjust your plan to stay on track and maintain momentum.

Stay disciplined and committed. Discipline and commitment are essential for overcoming adversity and staying focused on your goals. Develop healthy habits and routines that align with your objectives, and stay dedicated to your plan, even when the going gets tough.

Chapter #6 Overcoming Adversity and Thriving

Expert Advice from Psychologists and Life Coaches
"Adversity is a fact of life. It can't be controlled. What we can control is how we react to it." – Unknown

In this final section, we'll gather expert advice from psychologists and life coaches on overcoming adversity and thriving. Their wisdom and insights can provide invaluable guidance as you navigate the challenges and setbacks that life inevitably presents.

Embrace self-compassion. Dr. Kristin Neff, a leading researcher in self-compassion, emphasizes the importance of treating ourselves with kindness, understanding, and acceptance, particularly during difficult times. By practicing self-compassion, we can foster resilience and better navigate adversity.

Develop emotional intelligence. According to life coach and author Travis Bradberry, cultivating emotional intelligence is critical for overcoming adversity. By recognizing, understanding, and managing our emotions, we can improve our ability to cope with stress, make better decisions, and foster healthier relationships.

Chapter #6 Overcoming Adversity and Thriving

Practice mindfulness. Psychologist and author Dr. Jon Kabat-Zinn advocates for the practice of mindfulness as a means of building resilience and managing stress. By being present and fully engaged in the moment, we can develop greater self-awareness, emotional regulation, and mental clarity, allowing us to better handle adversity and thrive.

Overcoming adversity and thriving in the face of challenges requires resilience, a growth mindset, and a commitment to personal growth. By employing the strategies, tips, and expert advice shared in this chapter, you can develop the skills and mindset necessary to conquer life's obstacles, achieve your goals, and emerge stronger on the other side. Remember, adversity is an opportunity for growth and learning, and with the right mindset and support, you can overcome any challenge that comes your way. So embrace the power of a growth mindset, seek support when needed, stay focused on your goals, and draw inspiration from the stories of those who have triumphed over adversity. With perseverance, determination, and a belief in yourself, you can overcome any obstacle and thrive in the face of adversity.

Chapter 6 Workbook Activities:

Fill in the blanks:

A ____ mindset is the belief that our abilities and intelligence can be developed through dedication and hard work.

When overcoming adversity, it's important to ____ on your strengths and celebrate your accomplishments.

To stay focused on your goals, break them down into smaller, more achievable ____.

Surrounding yourself with a strong ____ network can help you navigate through tough times.

Multiple choice selection:
Which of the following is NOT a strategy for overcoming adversity?
a. Avoid seeking support from others
b. Maintain a positive attitude
c. Break challenges into smaller steps
d. Embrace failure as a learning opportunity

Journaling exercise:
Reflect on a recent challenge or setback you've faced. How did you react to the situation, and what could you have done differently to foster a growth mindset and demonstrate resilience?

Developing a growth mindset:
List three activities or experiences that could help you cultivate a growth mindset and foster a love for learning.

Overcoming adversity plan:
Identify a current challenge you're facing and create a realistic plan of action to overcome it. Break your plan down into smaller steps and outline the specific actions you'll take to achieve your goal.

Visualizing success:
Spend 5-10 minutes visualizing yourself achieving a specific goal or overcoming a challenge. Write down any emotions or insights that arise during the visualization exercise.

Chapter 7: Conclusion

Chapter 7: Conclusion

Welcome, young boss, to the end of our journey together. But fret not, for the adventure that awaits you in the real world is just beginning. In this climactic chapter, we'll recap the key strategies for thriving as a young man raised by a single parent. We'll also provide you with an action plan and goal-setting template, as well as additional resources to help you stay informed and inspired.

But first, allow me to present you with a round of applause, a pat on the back, and a hearty bear hug for making it this far. You've demonstrated your commitment to personal growth and taken a bold step toward a successful future. As the wise philosopher Confucius once said, "It does not matter how slowly you go, as long as you do not stop." So, young grasshopper, let's take a moment to reminisce on our epic journey and then charge forward to embrace your destiny.

Summary of Key Strategies for Thriving as a Young Man Raised by a Single Parent. Embrace Your Uniqueness: Remember, my friend, you are the rare gem in a world full of pebbles. By embracing your unique circumstances and appreciating the strength and resilience of your single parent, you're well on your way to becoming the best version of yourself.

Chapter 7: Conclusion

Cultivate a Strong Support System: Surround yourself with positive and empowering individuals who will encourage you to chase your dreams, provide guidance, and help you navigate through life's challenges. This support system can include friends, family members, mentors, coaches, and even online communities.

Develop Emotional Intelligence: Master the art of understanding, managing, and expressing your emotions, as well as empathizing with others. Emotional intelligence is key to building strong relationships, overcoming adversity, and achieving success in your personal and professional life.

Pursue Education and Personal Development. Feed your intellectual curiosity, explore new horizons, and invest in yourself through education and personal development. Acquiring new skills and knowledge not only makes you more marketable in the workforce but also enriches your life experiences.

Establish Financial Literacy: Learn the ins and outs of budgeting, saving, investing, and managing debt. Financial literacy empowers you to make informed decisions that will secure your financial future and help you achieve your goals.

Chapter 7: Conclusion

Set and Achieve Goals: Develop a clear vision of your future and establish SMART (Specific, Measurable, Achievable, Relevant, and Time-bound) goals. Break down your goals into smaller steps, stay disciplined, and celebrate your progress along the way.

Embrace Failure and Learn from It: Don't shy away from challenges or fear failure. Embrace it, learn from it, and use it as fuel to propel you forward. Remember, failure is merely a stepping stone on the road to success.

Now, it's time to take action and boss up for a successful future. To help you stay on track, we've created an action plan and goal-setting template. This template will assist you in applying the strategies discussed in this ebook and monitoring your progress over time.

Goal-Setting Template. Write down your goals: Clearly define your short-term and long-term goals, ensuring they are SMART. This will provide you with a roadmap to success.

Break down your goals. Divide your goals into smaller, manageable tasks or milestones. This will make them less overwhelming and help you maintain momentum.

Chapter 7: Conclusion

Set deadlines: Assign realistic deadlines to each task or milestone, and make sure to stick to them. This will keep you accountable and motivated to move forward.

Monitor your progress. Regularly evaluate your progress and make any necessary adjustments to your plan. This will ensure you stay on track and can adapt to any unforeseen obstacles.

Celebrate your achievements. Acknowledge and reward yourself for reaching milestones and achieving your goals. This will boost your confidence and reinforce the positive behaviors that lead to success.

As we bid adieu, remember that this is only the beginning In addition to our action plan and goal-setting template, we've compiled a list of resources to help you dive deeper into specific topics and expand your knowledge. These resources include articles, websites, and videos that are insightful, inspiring, and enlightening.

Chapter 7: Conclusion

Remember, your past does not dictate your future; with the right mindset and determination, you have the power to overcome challenges and create the life you desire. To support your journey, this chapter includes an action plan and goal-setting template to help you apply the strategies discussed in the ebook and track your progress over time. We also provide additional resources, such as links to relevant articles, websites, and videos, to supplement the content and offer readers access to more in-depth information on specific topics.

Made in the USA
Columbia, SC
11 June 2024